Dear Parent,

Thank you for investing your valuable family time in reading about our adventures in the Roo World. This series was designed to teach children that their actions have consequences. That is why our phrase "Think it through... Do the Roo" was developed. We all need to think before we act, and children especially need to understand that they are responsible for their behavior.

The concepts of safety, self esteem and respect are presented as additions to your vital nurturing. Keep in mind, these are only suggestions to give you guidance. Your family should determine what works best for you.

Children grow up so fast. We want them to be happy, but we need them to be safe.

Please, make safety "roo-teen".

Your roo-pal,
Pati Myers Gross

The Roo World Safety Seal

Home Safety is dedicated to all the moms, dads, grandparents, and caregivers who strive each day to create a safe and loving environment. It is also dedicated to the memory of my special Nana, Sadie Newfield, whose home was always filled with love, laughter, learning and encouragement.

I am proud to have been a member of the St. Petersburg, Florida Police Department, where I always received valuable training, guidance and support.

I would like to recognize a few of the many people who always encouraged me and believed in the Roo World concept: My husband, David, and children Michael and Steve; the entire Myers and Gross families; Lisa Smajovits; Sgt. Jeffrey A. Rink, Youth Resources Section, St. Petersburg. Florida Police Department; and a special thanks to George and Estelle Rosenfield.

Home Safety
by Pati Myers Gross

Author, Creator & Designer of Adventures in the Roo World: Pati Myers Gross.
Illustrator: Tom Gibson.
Editor: Carol Marger.

Adventures in the Roo World © Young Roo Series © Volume IV "Home Safety"
Published By
Roo Publications, St. Petersburg, Florida 33707
www.musicwithmar.com

Library of Congress Catalog Card Number: 98-68650. ISBN 0-9652579-4-0

Young Roo Series

Adventures in the Roo World

HOME SAFETY

RUNABOUT   **READER**   **RHYTHM**   **RAPPER**

Think it Through... Do the Roo!   Join the Hip Hop Mob.

A home is filled with laughter and joy;
It should be a safe place for every girl and boy.

But there are things in your house
you should handle with care.
Use your safety sense. Be alert. Be aware.

The Hip Hop Mob is checking Runabout's home,
Making sure it's safe as they roam.

Runabout chooses the kitchen to start the mission.
Join their adventure; it's a real expedition.

Sharp knives and scissors are for grown-ups to use.
Getting cut by these things will make you ooze.

Ovens and stoves are only used by Mom and Dad,
Because you can get burned and everyone
would be sad.

Never taste from a cleaning bottle.
There could be poison inside.
And then a trip to the hospital
would be your next ride.

Let's go to the bathroom and see what we find.
Think safety! Always keep it in mind.

Medicines can make us feel better when we're sick,
But only a grown-up knows which ones to pick.

Hot water is dangerous; your skin could burn.
Check the temperature first; this you must learn.

When getting clean in a bath, it's always fun to play,
And having an adult watch over you is the safest way.

Keeping your face under water isn't safe to do,
Especially if you want to be a hip hop roo.

Moms and dads use razors to shave
themselves neat,
But cutting yourself would be an awful trick,
not a treat.

Lighters and matches start fires quick as a wink.
They'll destroy a whole house before you can blink.

It's time for the Hip Hop Mob to check out the garage.
There's so much to be aware of;
it's a real hodge-podge.

There are poisonous chemicals and many sharp tools.
Kids who play with them are the real fools.

Washers, dryers, and cars are not meant to hide in.
No one may find you until you need
an ambulance to ride in.

An outlet provides electricity for a T.V., lamp, or clock,
But sticking something in it will give you quite a shock.

Climbing up high could result in a fumble;
both you and the furniture might take a terrible tumble.
Ask a grown-up for help; it's always a better way.
You'll end up having a much happier day.

If you ever answer the phone, don't give any secrets away.
Your mom and dad will tell you what is okay to say.

Kids can get shot by real guns they think are fake.
Staying away from ALL guns is good for safety's sake.

Swimming can be so much fun,
from a lake to a pool,
But never go in without an adult.
That's the rule.

This hip hop thumbs up is because you knew,
To Think it Through... Do the Roo!